DISCOVER
THE OCEANS

Atlantic Ocean

by Emily Rose Oachs

BLASTOFF!
3
READERS

BELLWETHER MEDIA • MINNEAPOLIS, MN

Note to Librarians, Teachers, and Parents:

Blastoff! Readers are carefully developed by literacy experts and combine standards-based content with developmentally appropriate text.

Level 1 provides the most support through repetition of high-frequency words, light text, predictable sentence patterns, and strong visual support.

Level 2 offers early readers a bit more challenge through varied simple sentences, increased text load, and less repetition of high-frequency words.

Level 3 advances early-fluent readers toward fluency through increased text and concept load, less reliance on visuals, longer sentences, and more literary language.

Level 4 builds reading stamina by providing more text per page, increased use of punctuation, greater variation in sentence patterns, and increasingly challenging vocabulary.

Level 5 encourages children to move from "learning to read" to "reading to learn" by providing even more text, varied writing styles, and less familiar topics.

Whichever book is right for your reader, Blastoff! Readers are the perfect books to build confidence and encourage a love of reading that will last a lifetime!

This edition first published in 2016 by Bellwether Media, Inc.

No part of this publication may be reproduced in whole or in part without written permission of the publisher. For information regarding permission, write to Bellwether Media, Inc., Attention: Permissions Department, 5357 Penn Avenue South, Minneapolis, MN 55419.

Library of Congress Cataloging-in-Publication Data

Oachs, Emily Rose.
  Atlantic Ocean / by Emily Rose Oachs.
     pages cm. – (Blastoff! Readers: Discover the Oceans)
  Summary: "Simple text and full-color photography introduce beginning readers to the Atlantic Ocean. Developed by literacy experts for students in kindergarten through third grade"—Provided by publisher.
  Audience: Ages 5-8.
  Audience: K to grade 3.
  Includes bibliographical references and index.
  ISBN 978-1-62617-331-6 (hardcover : alk. paper)
  1. Atlantic Ocean–Juvenile literature. I. Title.
  GC48.O33 2016
  910.9163–dc23

                              2015029933

Printed in the United States of America, North Mankato, MN.

Table of Contents

The Atlantic Ocean drains water from more land than any other ocean. Many of the world's major rivers connect to the Atlantic Ocean!

The mighty Amazon, Mississippi, and Congo rivers empty into the ocean's waters.

DID YOU KNOW?

- The Atlantic Ocean is saltier than any other ocean.

- In Canada's Bay of Fundy, the water level can change 53 feet (16 meters) in one day!

- In 1932, Amelia Earhart was the first woman to fly across the Atlantic Ocean alone. It took her 14 hours and 56 minutes!

- Mystery surrounds an area off Florida's coast called the Bermuda Triangle. Ships and airplanes have disappeared there.

Bay of Fundy

Where Is the Atlantic Ocean?

The **prime meridian** and **equator** divide the Atlantic Ocean. It is in all four **hemispheres**.

Atlantic waters flow into the Mediterranean and Caribbean seas. The western Atlantic borders North and South America. To the east lie Europe and Africa.

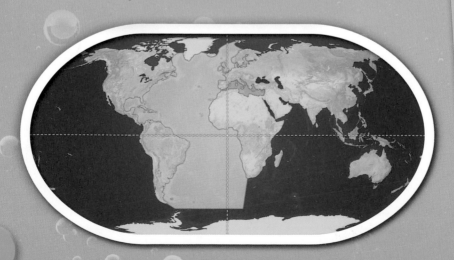

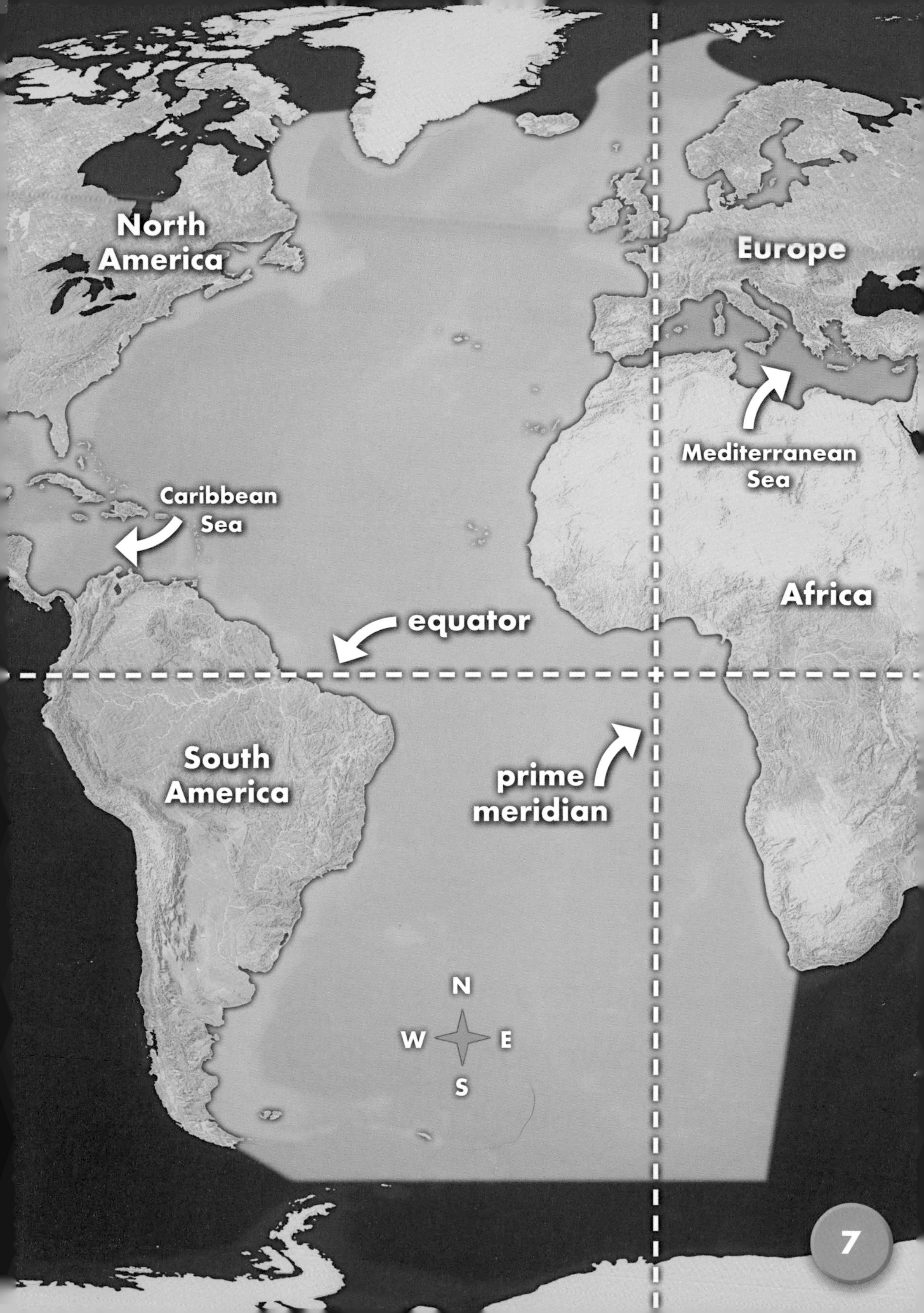

North
America

Europe

Mediterranean
Sea

Caribbean
Sea

Africa

equator

South
America

prime
meridian

N

W ✦ E

S

The Climate and Features

The Atlantic Ocean is cold in the far north and south. The water is warmer near the equator.

Currents move warm and cold water through the Atlantic Ocean. They carry the ocean's water in large loops.

surface
currents

→ warm

→ cold

hurricane

Hurricanes form in late summer. They often hit the Caribbean islands and southeastern United States.

In chilly waters, **icebergs** drift. Natural gas and oil are below much of the ocean floor.

Mid-Atlantic Ridge

The Mid-Atlantic Ridge is an underwater mountain range. The mountains stretch for 10,000 miles (16,000 kilometers). They trail down the center of the ocean.

Mid-Atlantic Ridge

Mountains may rise above
the ocean's surface. These
form islands.

Earthquakes shake the Mid-Atlantic Ridge. Sometimes underwater **volcanoes** shoot **lava** into the ocean!

Some islands are made of cooled lava.

Canary
Islands

phytoplankton

Tiny **phytoplankton** drift near the Atlantic Ocean's surface. Seaweed clumps float in the Sargasso Sea.

**kelp
forest**

Groups of **kelp** grow close
to shore in the ocean's
cool waters. They make
underwater forests.

right whale

Each summer, right whales **migrate** north. They search for food.

Sea stars and angelfish hide in **coral reefs**. Giant squid and harp seals swim in the icy north. The Atlantic Ocean is home to many different life forms!

sea stars

angelfish

giant squid

harp seal

Fast Facts About the Atlantic Ocean

Size: 29.6 million square miles (76.8 million square kilometers); 2nd largest ocean

Average Depth: 10,925 feet (3,330 meters)

Greatest Depth: 27,493 feet (8,380 meters)

Major Bodies of Water: Caribbean Sea, Gulf of Mexico, Sargasso Sea, Labrador Sea, Mediterranean Sea

Continents Touched: North America, South America, Africa, Europe

Total Coastline: 69,510 miles (111,866 kilometers)

Top Natural Resources: coal, gravel, natural gas, oil, seals, whales

Famous Shipwrecks:
- *San Marcos* (1588)
- RMS *Titanic* (1912)
- RMS *Lusitania* (1915)
- *Bismarck* (1941)

RMS *Titanic*

North
America

Labrador
Sea

Europe

Gulf of
Mexico

Sargasso
Sea

Mediterranean
Sea

Caribbean
Sea

Africa

Atlantic
Ocean

South
America

N

W   E

S

Glossary

coral reefs—structures made of coral that usually grow in shallow seawater

currents—large patterns of water movement in an ocean

earthquakes—disasters in which the ground shakes because of the movement of rock deep underground

equator—an imaginary line around the center of Earth; the equator divides the planet into a northern half and a southern half.

hemispheres—halves of the globe; the equator and prime meridian divide Earth into different hemispheres.

hurricanes—windy, swirling storms that form over warm water; hurricanes bring rain, wind, thunder, and lightning.

icebergs—large pieces of floating ice in the ocean

kelp—a large seaweed

lava—hot, melted rock that flows out of an active volcano

migrate—to travel from one place to another, often with the seasons

phytoplankton—tiny ocean plants that drift

prime meridian—an imaginary line that runs vertically around Earth; the prime meridian divides the planet into a western half and an eastern half.

volcanoes—holes in the earth; when a volcano erupts, hot, melted rock called lava shoots out.

To Learn More

AT THE LIBRARY

Burleigh, Robert. *Night Flight: Amelia Earhart Crosses the Atlantic.* New York, N.Y.: Simon & Schuster Books for Young Readers, 2011.

Dubowski, Mark. *Titanic: The Disaster that Shocked the World!* New York, N.Y.: DK Publishing, 2015.

Spilsbury, Louise and Richard. *Atlantic Ocean.* Chicago, Ill.: Capstone Heinemann Library, 2015.

ON THE WEB

Learning more about the Atlantic Ocean is as easy as 1, 2, 3.

1. Go to www.factsurfer.com.

2. Enter "Atlantic Ocean" into the search box.

3. Click the "Surf" button and you will see a list of related web sites.

With factsurfer.com, finding more information is just a click away.

Index

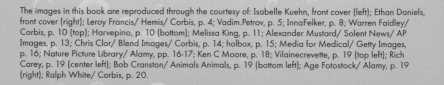